TERRIFIC TEAMS

Meet the LOS ANGELES DODGERS

PERCY LEED

Lerner Publications ◆ Minneapolis

Stats in this book are accurate through the 2024 Major League Baseball season.

Lerner Publications Company
An imprint of Lerner Publishing Group, Inc.
241 First Avenue North
Minneapolis, MN 55401 USA

For reading levels and more information, look up this title at www.lernerbooks.com.

Main body text set in ITC Avant Garde Gothic Std.
Typeface provided by Adobe Systems.

Editor: Elena Mai **Designer:** Martha Kranes **Photo Editor:** Evan Villas

Library of Congress Cataloging-in-Publication Data

Names: Leed, Percy, 1968- author
Title: Meet the Los Angeles Dodgers / Percy Leed.
Description: Minneapolis, Minnesota : Lerner Publications, [2026] | Series: Lerner Sports Rookie. Terrific teams | Includes bibliographical references and index. | Audience: Ages 5–8 | Audience: Grades 2–3 | Summary: "The Los Angeles Dodgers won their eighth World Series title in 2024. Discover the team's history, legendary players, thrilling wins, incredible stats and more in this fun, exciting book"— Provided by publisher.
Identifiers: LCCN 2025015089 (print) | LCCN 2025015090 (ebook) | ISBN 9798765689677 lib. bdg. | ISBN 9798348029432 pbk. | ISBN 9798765699348 epub
Subjects: LCSH: Los Angeles Dodgers (Baseball team)—History | Brooklyn Dodgers (Baseball team)—History | World Series (Baseball)—History
Classification: LCC GV875.B7 L44 2026 (print) | LCC GV875.B7 (ebook) | DDC 796.357/640979494—dc23/eng/20250530

LC record available at https://lccn.loc.gov/2025015089
LC ebook record available at https://lccn.loc.gov/2025015090

Manufactured in the United States of America
1-1012408-54835-6/23/2025

Photo Acknowledgments
Image credits: Elsa/Getty Images, p. 5; Kevork Djansezian/Getty Images, p. 7; Bettmann/Getty Images, pp. 9, 13–14; Maddie Meyer/Getty Images, p. 11; Cooper Neill/MLB Photos via Getty Images, p. 16; Al Bello/Getty Images, p. 18; Leon Bennett/WireImage, p. 20; Wally Skalij / Los Angeles Times via Getty Images, p. 22; Kyodo News via Getty Images, p. 23. Design elements: Kwangmoozaa/Getty Images; Andrii Shelenkov/Getty Images; jasonclardy/Getty Images. Cover: AP Photo/Kyodo.

Table of Contents

Chapter 1 Eight-Time Champions 4

Chapter 2 Big Moments 8

Chapter 3 Best Players 12

Chapter 4 Dodgers Blue 19

Los Angeles Dodgers Team Leaders 23

Glossary 24

Learn More 24

Index 24

★ CHAPTER 1 ★

Eight-Time Champions

In October 2024, Walker Buehler pitched for the Los Angeles Dodgers. The New York Yankees batter missed the ball three times. Strikeout!

The Dodgers won the 2024 World Series!

The Dodgers and their fans celebrated the win. They had a parade in Los Angeles, California.

The Dodgers have won the World Series eight times.

★ CHAPTER 2 ★

Big Moments

The Dodgers began in Brooklyn, New York. They were first known as the Brooklyn Dodgers. In 1958, they moved to Los Angeles.

Between 1955 and 1988, the Dodgers won the World Series six times.

The Dodgers won the World Series again in 2020. They beat the Tampa Bay Rays in six games.

In the 2024 World Series, the Dodgers beat the Yankees in five games. It was the Dodgers' fourth World Series win against the Yankees.

★ CHAPTER 3 ★

Best Players

In 1947, Jackie Robinson joined the Dodgers. He was the first Black player in MLB in more than 50 years.

Robinson helped the Dodgers win their first World Series in 1955.

Sandy Koufax is one of the best pitchers in Dodgers history.

He helped the Dodgers
win four World Series.

The Cy Young Award is given to the best pitchers in MLB. Clayton Kershaw won three Cy Young Awards.

In 2024, Shohei Ohtani was named the MVP of the NL.

Ohtani is the first MLB player to hit 50 home runs and steal 50 bases in a single season.

★ CHAPTER 4 ★

Dodgers Blue

The Dodgers have played home games at Dodger Stadium since 1962.

In 2017, the Dodgers built a statue of Jackie Robinson. It stands at Dodger Stadium.

The team made changes to Dodger Stadium for the 2025 season. It has bigger spaces for fans to enjoy.

Fans hope to see Los Angeles win another World Series soon!

LOS ANGELES DODGERS TEAM LEADERS

Batting average:	Willie Keeler, .352
Hits:	Zack Wheat, 2,804
Home runs:	Duke Snider, 389
Wins:	Don Sutton, 233
Strikeouts:	Clayton Kershaw, 2,968

Glossary

MLB: Major League Baseball

MVP: Most Valuable Player

NL: National League

Learn More

Leed, Percy. *Baseball's World Series*. Lerner Publications, 2025.

Marino Walters, Jennifer. *Jackie Robinson: Baseball's Second-Base Hero*. Red Chair Press, 2025.

Tischler, Joe. *Shohei Ohtani*. Amicus Learning, 2025.

Index

Dodger Stadium, 19–21

Koufax, Sandy, 14

New York Yankees, 4, 11

Robinson, Jackie, 12–13, 20

World Series, 5, 7, 9–11, 13, 15, 22